Swans

*written and photographed
by Lynn M. Stone*

Lerner Publications Company • Minneapolis, Minnesota

For my parents
  —LMS

Photographs in this book were taken in Essex, Connecticut; Rockford, Minnesota; Michigan State University's Kellogg Bird Sanctuary; Chicago Zoological Park (Brookfield Zoo); Pocosin Lakes National Wildlife Refuge in North Carolina; LaPerouse Bay in Manitoba, Canada; Fermi National Accelerator Laboratory in Illinois; National Elk Refuge in Montana; and Yellowstone National Park in Wyoming.

Thanks to our series consultant, Sharyn Fenwick, elementary science/math specialist. Mrs. Fenwick was the winner of the National Science Teachers Association 1991 Distinguished Teaching Award. She also was the recipient of the Presidential Award for Excellence in Math and Science Teaching, representing the state of Minnesota at the elementary level in 1992.

Early Bird Nature Books were conceptualized by Ruth Berman and designed by Steve Foley. Series editor is Joelle Goldman.

Library of Congress Cataloging-in-Publication Data

Stone, Lynn M.
  Swans / written and photographed by Lynn M. Stone.
    p. cm. – (Early bird nature books)
  Includes index.
  Summary: Describes the physical characteristics, behavior, life cycle, and habitat of the swan.
  ISBN 0-8225-3019-8 (alk. paper)
  1. Swans—Juvenile literature. [1. Swans.] I. Title. II. Series.
QL696.A52S78 1997
598.4'1—DC20   96-27707

Manufactured in the United States of America
1 2 3 4 5 6 – SP – 02 01 00 99 98 97

Contents

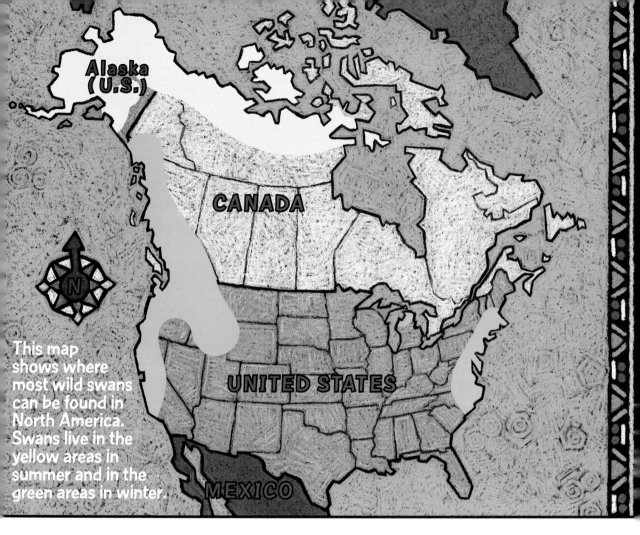

Alaska
(U.S.)

CANADA

UNITED STATES

MEXICO

This map shows where most wild swans can be found in North America. Swans live in the yellow areas in summer and in the green areas in winter.

Be a Word Detective

Can you find these words as you read about the swan's life? Be a detective and try to figure out what they mean. You can turn to the glossary on page 47 for help.

bill	flight feathers	omnivores
clutch	habitat	predators
cygnets	incubate	preen
down	migration	tundra

Chapter 1

Baby swans are not "ugly ducklings." What birds are related to swans?

Big, Beautiful Swans

Almost everyone knows the swan. Remember the story of the ugly duckling? In the story, the ugly little duckling becomes a big, beautiful swan.

The world has thousands of swans. Some swans live in captivity, which means that people keep them. But most swans are wild.

Swans are related to ducks and geese. Ducks, geese, and swans all live on water. Swans are the biggest of these waterbirds.

This white bird is a swan. It is bigger than the geese nearby.

There are eight species, or kinds, of swans. Wild swans live nearly all around the world. But no wild swans live in Africa or Antarctica.

Most swans are white when they are adults. The swans of North America are all white. But Australia has black swans. And South America has black-necked swans.

Black-necked swans live in South America.

*Black swans come from Australia. Like all swans,
black swans are graceful swimmers.*

Trumpeter swans (left) and tundra *swans (below)* both *swim with their necks straight up. Tundra swans have a yellow spot on their bills.*

North America has three species of wild swans. They are the trumpeter swan, the tundra swan, and the mute swan. These swans all live in the northern part of North America.

There is an easy way to tell North America's swans apart. Their bills, or beaks, are different. Trumpeter swans have black bills. Tundra swans have black bills, too. But their bills have a yellow spot near the bird's eyes. Mute swans have orange bills.

Mute swans swim with their necks in an S shape. Their orange bills have a black knob near the bird's eyes.

Tundra swans call loudly as they fly.

Different species of swans have different voices. Trumpeter swans make loud calls like a trumpet. Tundra swans make loud calls like geese. But mute swans don't make loud calls. The word *mute* means unable to speak. Mute swans can only grunt and hiss.

Trumpeter and tundra swans have lived in North America for thousands of years. Mute swans first came to North America in the 1800s. People brought them from Europe as captive birds. Some of these captive swans escaped. They raised families in the wild. Soon many mute swans in North America were wild.

This mute swan is wild. Mute swans can weigh 30 pounds.

Chapter 2

A marsh is a good place for swans to live. What are some other places where wild swans can live?

Life on the Water

Swans spend most of their lives on water or near water. They often live on shallow lakes or ponds. Some swans live in marshes. The places where a swan can live are called its habitats.

Tundra swans are born on the arctic tundra. The tundra is an area in the far north. The ground there is frozen most of the year. In summer, the tundra has many shallow ponds.

This nest belongs to tundra swans. It is on the tundra in Canada.

Swans were made for life on the water.
They float easily. They have wide, webbed feet.
Their feet help them paddle across the water.

A swan's webbed feet are good for paddling.

Swans have warm, waterproof feathers.

A swan's feathers are waterproof. The feathers also keep the bird warm. That's because feathers trap air. Then the bird's body heats the air.

*Water rolls right off
a swan's waterproof
feathers.*

*Swans lose their
feathers every
summer. Then they
grow new ones.*

This swan is preening. Swans preen their feathers every day.

To take care of their feathers, swans preen. When a swan preens, it uses its bill to smooth its feathers. A swan's body makes a special oil. Preening spreads the oil on the swan's feathers. The oil makes the feathers waterproof.

This swan is looking for underwater plants.

Swans are omnivores (AHM-nih-vorz). Omnivores are animals who eat both plants and animals.

Swans eat mostly underwater plants. But swans can't dive. So they feed where the water is shallow. In shallow water, plants are near the surface. Swans dip their necks underwater to find this food.

Sometimes a swan wants to reach plants in deeper water. Then the swan thrusts its long neck straight down. Its tail tilts up in the air, like a seesaw.

A swan reaches deep to get tubers, a kind of plant root. Tubers are buried in the water's muddy bottom.

A swan keeps its head underwater for just a few seconds. That's enough time to find plant snacks. A swan's bill is large and powerful. It has sharp edges like a scissors. It cuts plants quickly and easily.

Swans don't eat only plants. They eat insects, too. Some swans eat small, hard-shelled animals, such as clams.

A swan tears off plants with its sharp bill.

Chapter 3

These eggs belong to trumpeter swans. At what time of year do swans lay their eggs?

Swan Families

Swans live together for much of the year. They eat and travel in groups called flocks. But in spring, the flocks break up. Spring is the time when swans lay eggs.

To get ready to lay eggs, pairs of swans go off on their own. A pair has two adult swans. One swan is a male, and one is a female. Once swans form a pair, they stay together for life.

This pair of trumpeter swans has built a nest near the water.

Male and female swans look alike. Females sit on the nest.

Each pair chooses a place to build a nest. Swans build their nests on the shore, or on little islands. Swans build large nests. They make their nests out of plants. Then they line the nest with a few feathers.

The female swan lays eggs in the nest. A mother swan usually lays five or six eggs. A group of eggs is called a clutch.

This mother swan has gotten up to stretch.

If eggs get too hot or too cold, the babies inside will die. So the mother incubates (ING-kyoo-baits), or sits on, the eggs. Incubating keeps the eggs at the right temperature. Now and then the mother gets up to stretch or to eat.

The father swan guards the nest. He keeps other swans away. He scares off animals who might eat the eggs.

In four or five weeks, the eggs hatch. Baby swans are called cygnets (SIHG-nehts). Some newborn birds are naked. But not cygnets. They are covered with down when they hatch. Down is a kind of feather. Down feathers are warm and fluffy.

These baby swans are covered with down feathers.

After cygnets hatch, they stay in the nest for a day or two. Then their parents lead them out onto the water. Cygnets can swim right away.

Mother swans and father swans both stay close to their babies.

Baby swans watch their parents to learn how to find food.

Cygnets can feed themselves right away, too. They learn how to find food by watching their parents. Some swan babies eat mostly insects at first. Insects are easier to munch than plants. When the cygnets are about two weeks old, they are strong enough to tear off plants.

Most young swans are gray until their adult feathers grow in. Like adult swans, young swans preen their feathers.

Cygnets can't fly. That's because they don't have flight feathers. These are the straight, stiff feathers that help birds fly. Flight feathers grow on a bird's wings and tail.

Swan families stay mostly on the water. On the shore, there are many predators (PREH-duh-turz). Predators are animals who hunt other animals. Most predators won't bother adult swans. But they will eat baby swans. So cygnets are safer on the water.

This mink could eat a baby swan. Coyotes, foxes, raccoons, weasels, owls, gulls, and snapping turtles also hunt swans.

Mother and father swans watch their babies closely. If danger appears, the parents call to the cygnets. Then the family hides among water plants. Or they swim far away from shore.

This swan parent is stretching its wings. A swan's wings may spread 8 feet from tip to tip.

These young swans will have all their flight feathers by the end of the summer.

By late summer, most young swans have grown flight feathers. They stretch their wings and soon learn to fly.

Young swans stay with their parents for a year or more. By the time young swans are three years old, they are ready to start a family of their own.

Chapter 4

Tundra swans fly south for the winter. Do all swans have different winter and summer homes?

Swan Travels

In the fall, most swans gather in flocks again. Then they fly together to warmer places. In the spring, they return to their nesting places. Each trip is called a migration.

Not all swans migrate. In North America, mute swans stay close to their nesting places all year.

Migrating swans go to the same winter homes each year. They follow the same routes. They probably use the sun, the moon, and the stars to guide them. Young swans learn the way from adults.

To fly, swans need a running start. They run across the water before they take off.

Tundra swans make the longest trips.
Some tundra swans travel from northern
Canada to North Carolina. They travel more
than 2,000 miles.

Swans usually fly at night. But sometimes they fly during the day.

These tundra swans have stopped to feed in a farmer's field.

Swans can fly hundreds of miles before they need to rest. When they stop, they may rest in one place for several weeks.

Flocks of swans often fly in the shape of a V. *They may fly as high as 2 miles above the earth.*

Swans can fly faster than a horse can run. When swans fly with the wind, they can go even faster. But when swans fly against the wind, the wind slows them down.

Migration is not easy. Flying against the wind makes the birds tired. Cloudy skies can make them lose their way. Sometimes swans have accidents. In foggy weather, they may fly into wires.

A young swan's first migration is especially hard. Many young swans are not strong enough to finish the trip. They die along the way.

The long migration of tundra swans may take three months. At the trip's end, the youngest swans are only five or six months old.

These tundra swans have arrived at their winter home in North Carolina.

Chapter 5

People once hunted trumpeter swans for their feathers. What did people do with the feathers?

Saving Swans

Many years ago, people hunted trumpeter swans for their meat and feathers. People used the flight feathers to decorate women's hats. They used the down feathers to stuff mattresses and pillows.

Soon, few trumpeters were left. In some nesting places, there were none. Then people decided to protect the trumpeters. They made laws against hunting trumpeters.

Tundra swans nest far from most people. So few tundra swans were killed. Mute swans were safe, too. During much of the hunting, most mute swans lived in captivity. Hunters weren't allowed to shoot them.

These trumpeter swans have found a safe home near Yellowstone National Park.

Swans still face danger from people. People have drained many ponds and marshes. There is land where water used to be. People have moved into these places. So swans have fewer places to live.

To help swans, people have set aside safe places for them to live. One place is Yellowstone National Park.

People can find ways to share swan habitats with wild swans.

Wild swans still fly across North America.

People also help swans in another way. Each year people take trumpeters to places where these swans used to nest. Trumpeters have started nesting in those places again.

Swans are doing well. More swans live in North America now than when your grandparents were young. Watch for these big birds. On the water or in the air, swans are a beautiful sight.

On Sharing a Book

As you know, adults greatly influence a child's attitude toward reading. When a child sees you read, or when you share a book with a child, you're sending a message that reading is important. Show the child that reading a book together is important to you. Find a comfortable, quiet place. Turn off the television and limit other distractions such as telephone calls.

Be prepared to start slowly. Take turns reading parts of this book. Stop and talk about what you're reading. Talk about the photographs. You may find that much of the shared time is spent discussing just a few pages. This discussion time is valuable for both of you, so don't move through the book too quickly. If the child begins to lose interest, stop reading. Continue sharing the book at another time. When you do pick up the book again, be sure to revisit the parts you have already read. Most importantly, enjoy the book!

Be a Vocabulary Detective

You will find a word list on page 5. Words selected for this list are important to the understanding of the topic of this book. Encourage the child to be a word detective and search for the words as you read the book together. Talk about what the words mean and how they are used in the sentence. Do any of these words have more than one meaning? You will find these words defined in a glossary on page 47.

What about Questions?

Use questions to make sure the child understands the information in this book. Here are some suggestions:

> What did this paragraph tell us? What does this picture show? What do you think we'll learn about next? Are all swans white? Tell me about the places where swans can live. Could a swan live in your backyard? Why/Why not? How do swans find their food? Where do swans build their nests? What enemies do swans have? How do mother and father swans take care of their babies? What swans make the longest migrations? How high can swans fly? How do people help swans? What is your favorite part of the book? Why?

If the child has questions, don't hesitate to respond with questions of your own such as: What do *you* think? Why? What is it that you don't know? If the child can't remember certain facts, turn to the index.

Introducing the Index

The index is an important learning tool. It helps readers get information quickly without searching throughout the whole book. Turn to the index on page 48. Choose an entry such as *preening,* and ask the child to use the index to find out why swans preen. Repeat this exercise with as many entries as you like. Ask the child to point out the differences between an index and a glossary. (An index helps readers find information quickly, while a glossary tells readers what words mean.)

Where in the World?

Many plants and animals found in the Early Bird Nature Books series live in parts of the world other than the United States. Encourage the child to find the places mentioned in this book on a world map or globe. Take time to talk about climate, terrain, and how you might live in such places.

All the World in Metric

Although our monetary system is in metric units (based on multiples of 10), the United States is one of the few countries in the world that does not use the metric system of measurement. Here are some conversion activities you and the child can do using a calculator:

WHEN YOU KNOW:	MULTIPLY BY:	TO FIND:
miles	1.609	kilometers
feet	0.3048	meters
inches	2.54	centimeters
pounds	0.454	kilograms

Activities

Read the story of the ugly duckling. Talk about the story. In what ways is the baby swan in the story like the baby swans in this book? How is the baby swan in the story different?

Have the child make up a story about swans. Be sure information from this book is included. Have the child illustrate the story.

Visit a zoo to see swans. What kinds of swans are there? What are the differences among the swans at the zoo? How are swans similar to other birds at the zoo? How are they different?

Glossary

bill—a bird's beak

clutch—a group of eggs

cygnets (SIHG-nehts)—baby swans

down—soft, fluffy feathers

flight feathers—stiff feathers that help a bird to fly

habitat—an area where a kind of animal can live and grow

incubate (ING-kyoo-bait)—to sit on eggs and keep them the right temperature so they'll hatch

migration—the trip back and forth between a swan's summer home and its winter home

omnivores (AHM-nih-vorz)—animals who eat both plants and animals

predators (PREH-duh-turz)—animals who hunt and eat other animals

preen—to smooth feathers with a bill

tundra—a place in the far north where the ground is frozen almost all year

Index

Pages listed in **bold** type refer to photographs.